THE CULTURE OF ROYAL CIVILITY

Professor Julian Businge
&
Sir Clyde Rivers

Copyright © 2020 Julian Businge &
Sir Clyde Rivers

All rights reserved. No part of this publication may be reproduced, distributed, or transmitted in any form or by any means, including photocopying, recording, or any other electronic or mechanical methods, without the prior written permission of the publisher, except in the case of brief quotations embodied in critical reviews and certain other noncommercial uses permitted by copyright law. For permission, write to the publisher at the address below:

Greatness University Publishers London
www.greatnessuniversity.co.uk

ISBN: 978-1-913164-39-3
ISBN-13: 978-1-913164-39-3

DEDICATION

To you who is seeking to deliver your royalty.

CONTENTS

Introduction	3
Preface	5
Divine Royalty	11
Chapter One: The Culture of Royal Civility	15
Chapter Two: What is Kingdom on Earth?	25
Chapter Three: Born to Reign	37
Chapter Four: Principles of a Kingdom	43
Chapter Five: How to live in a Kingdom	49
Chapter Six: Royal Protocol	57
Chapter Seven: The Principle of Management	65
Chapter Eight: Royal Civility Quotes	71
Chapter Nine: Global Initiative	77
Conclusion	85
About the Authors	89

THERE IS ROYALTY IN YOU

INTRODUCTION

We are happy to bring you a teaching that can bring a definite change of mentality in you and prompt you to take a new step in your spiritual journey OF DISCOVERING YOUR TRUE IDENTITY. It's going to be between the Sovereignty of God and Sovereignty of man. Let's take a look at what the Bible says about Royalty. According to 1 Peter 2:9, But you are a chosen generation, a Royal priesthood, a Holy nation, a peculiar people; that ye should shew forth the praises of him who hath called you out of darkness into his marvelous light.

Everyone on the Earth is born with significance and purpose. Since the creation of the world, the Almighty God has created billions of people, and the current world population has 7.8 billion people representing his kingdom of God on Earth. God's plan in creation of man is to extend his family on Earth. He created man like him with the same DNA and made him the King of the Earth to take dominion (to be in-charge). May God be Glorified in every area of your lives as we walk in our divine Royalty.

God is so perfect and he will never make mistakes. He loves us all without discrimination and has commanded us to have dominion, be fruitful and multiply. Therefore, it's our heritage and God's will for us to advance his kingdom on Earth and leave a legacy.

Anybody born into the world has a crown. For instance, the modern-day Kings and Queens are first class citizen in any country or society. Our ideas are our inheritance bringing solutions to the world. We belong in the God Class.

This is the right time for the Royal giant to arise in you and crush the inner critic. Identity crisis is the lack of knowing who we are.

The Culture of Royal Civility

PREFACE

ROYALTY

We are a Royal priesthood this is our inheritance. There are two concepts of Royalty, which are the earthly Kings and kingdoms and the Heavenly kingdom of God, The Kings of Kings.

When it comes to earthly Royalty, it simply means the members of a Royal family. A Royal family is the immediate family of a King, Queen, Regnant, Emirs, and sometimes an extended family.

When thinking about modern day Kings and Queens, for example, Queen Elizabeth II, The Queen of England, is the first that comes to mind with the longest reigning monarch and most powerful kingdom so far.

There are more than 29 modern day monarchies, reigning globally. Some, like King Salam bin Abdulaziz Al of Saudi Arabia rule absolutely, An Absolute Monarchy is a form of government that involved the society being ruled over by an all-powerful King or Queen in control over all aspects of the society, including: political power, economics, and all forms of authority while others, such as King Willem-Alexander of the Netherlands, serve more as ambassadors for their country's governments.

Others still are not even Kings or Queens, but rather princes reigning over principalities, like Albert II of

Monaco or grand dukes over dukedoms, like the one in Luxembourg. Some African kings rule cultural kingdoms, while others are both government and cultural leaders.

A Monarch is simply the head of a monarchy, a type of government in which a state is ruled by an individual for a long period of time or until abdication, and the person is usually inheriting the throne by birth right. In other words, a monarch could be autocrats or may be ceremonial figureheads, exercising only limited or no reserve powers at all, with actual authority given in a legislature or executive cabinet. This can be found in many constitutional monarchies.

Sometimes, a monarch can also be linked with a state religion. And most states only have a single monarch at any given time, although a regent may rule when the monarch is a minor, not present or unable to rule. This really happens when two monarchs rule simultaneously over a single state, such as what's happening in Andorra, which is known as coregencies.

Andorra is the world's only co-principality. A principality is a place ruled by a prince. Monaco is an example of a principality. Andorra, however, is a co-principality. They have two princes who jointly share the title of prince. Surprisingly, neither of the two princes are from Andorra. One prince is the President of France, Emmanuel Macron. The other co-prince is the Bishop of Urgell, who is currently Joan Enric Vives Sicília. The position is a constitutional one similar to the British Monarchy and holds no real power. Except for limited things, the two princes must exercise their authority together, not separately. This is the only country where one of their heads of state, the President of France is democratically elected by another country. The other prince, the bishop, is appointed by the head of state of another country usually the Pope.

Titles and styles are what distinguished monarchs, which in most cases are defined by tradition, and guaranteed under the state's constitution. Divers of titles are applied in English, for instance, "King" and "Queen", "Prince" and "Princess", "Emperor" and "Empress."

However, each of them will be addressed differently in their local languages. The names and titles have been styled using the common English equivalent. Roman numerals, used to distinguish related rulers with the same name, have been applied where typical. But in socio-cultural and political studies, monarchies are usually associated with hereditary rule; most monarchs, both historical and contemporary contexts, have been born and raised within a Royal family.

Succession has been explained using a variety of distinct formulae, like proximity of blood, primogeniture and agnatic seniority. Although, some monarchies aren't hereditary, and the ruler is instead determined through an elective process, these are very few.

A good modern example is the throne of Malaysia. Such systems defy the model concept of a monarchy but are commonly referred to such because they retain associative characteristics. Most systems use a combination of hereditary and also an elective element, where the election of a successor is restricted to members of a Royal bloodline.

Royal Titles

Highness - In some countries, they address their Royal person as Highness. (Your Highness, My Highness, Her Highness, etc.)

King, Male, Monarch, Rex- This is a male sovereign ruler of a Kingdom.

Prince - Usually a male member of a Royal family other than the sovereign is the son of a sovereign.

Princess - This is a female member of a Royal family other than the Queen is especially the daughter of a sovereign.

The Authority is in the head that is the King or Queen ruling at the time. Kingdoms generally dominate a territory with its cultures and social wellbeing. The power of the ruler is unchangeable and final. A king cannot be voted out of power and serves for life.

The King's authority is delegated through his name and he can delegate authority to act in his name or on his behalf. In a kingdom, the king owns everything; there is no personal ownership, only stewardship over the king's property in a kingdom, the king has a realm and a reign.

Learning the backgrounds and characteristics of the ruling kingdoms for example in the United Kingdom, helps us relate with Gods kingdom in Heaven and how to carry and handle ourselves as Royalty.

The Culture of Royal Civility

PROLOGUE

DIVINE ROYALTY

We are the Royal Family of God. God in Heaven is SOVEREIGN. Understanding the sovereignty of God is extremely important. Here are a few insights in hope of bringing some clarity, or at least what I believe is clarity to this subject. The way I like to explain God's sovereignty best is simply to say, "God is the King of Kings." If you were to look up the word "sovereign" in the dictionary, you would find words and phrases like "superior," "greatest," "supreme in power and authority," "ruler," and "independent of all others" in its definition.

There is absolutely nothing that happens in the universe that is outside of God's influence and authority. As King of kings and Lord of Lords, God has no limitations. Consider just a few of the claims the Bible makes about God.

According to Revelation 21:6, God is above all things and before all things. He is the Alpha and the Omega, the beginning, and the end. He is immortal, and He is present everywhere so that everyone can know Him. This great God created all things and holds all things together, both in heaven and on earth, both visible and invisible (Colossians 1:16).

Our God knows everything, the past, present and future. O the depth of the riches both of the wisdom and knowledge of God! How unsearchable are his judgements, and his ways past finding out (Romans

11:33) KJV. God can do all things and accomplish all things. Nothing is too difficult for Him and He orchestrates and determines everything that is going to happen in your life, in my life, in America and throughout the world. Whatever He wants to do in the universe, He does, for nothing is impossible with Him.

God is in control of all things and rules over all things. He has power and authority over nature, earthly kings, history, angels, and demons. Even Satan himself has to ask God's permission before he can act (Psalm 103:19). That is what being sovereign means. It means being the ultimate source of all power, authority, and everything that exists.

Only God can make those claims; therefore, it's God's sovereignty that makes Him superior to all other kings and makes Him and Him alone. We call him Father and therefore automatic Royals of an everlasting kingdom. None of us gets to heaven by our merit. Neither do we receive victory, blessings, love or son-ship by merit. We would all fall short of deserving anything. Instead, we are invited to freely receive the free gift of Christ's merit.

Because Christ is our brother, Romans 8, tells us we get to receive everything He has, like heirs and heiresses; we are seated with Christ in Heavenly places therefore royalty. It's all God's grace to humanity.

Chapter One

THE CULTURE OF ROYAL CIVILITY

A Royal culture gives a sense of belonging and direction and is important to share experiences, grow and strengthen the people. The culture has characteristics of a way of life and communication that is desirable to others. How you speak, dress (dress according to how you want to be addressed), how you think, your manners /etiquette, and your God kind of language are things that describe who you are and where you belong.

Now, let's look at the definition of "Royal Civility." Royal Civility is simply means we are Kings and priests using our gifts at a high level to help humanity. We lead with our gifts and everyone's gift is a solution to someone else's problem. Nobody is a no body in the kingdom of God. He has made us all in His image.

A man's gift makes room for him, and brings him before great men. God gave you gift to prosper in everything. If you have a special gift and you are not working to develop it, you will see it going down the drain. Gifts are very powerful; they are a man's destiny and only hope. If you ask the Holy Spirit for direction or ideas, he will give you the ideas, He will tell you what work to do so that you can prosper with your gifts but you have to work hard.

The very power that makes opportunities, that makes money that creates new things, that brings together things that others have created but were unable to utilise is inside of you. "A man's gift will makes room for him" Jesus Christ said, My Father is working hitherto and I work too. If you don't want to work hard then don't ask for financial breakthrough. There is a difference between magic and miracle. My Father is a miracle worker not a magician (Proverbs 18:16).

The real truth and principles of Royalty are Kings and Priests co-existing together. Kings can be referred to as our leaders in politics, government, cultural and traditional leaders and family leaders. Priests are our religious leaders or spiritual leaders. They work together to make sure there is positive change in our community.

The current 7.8 billion people living in the world are born with a gift meant to solve the different problems in the world when we all connect to the power of God within us. Everyone's assignment comes with a gift which gives us authority. Everyone's diversity is respected and honoured.

The safe place of creating opportunity to bring contribution to the world is through the "Culture of Royal Civility." The word "Royal" means 'Kingly'. The duties and responsibilities of Kings are to govern the affairs of the people. It is a priesthood that has been elevated to rule and exercise a priestly function in coordination with their High Priest, the King of Kings. It is a priesthood that is entrusted with authority to rule and reign with Him.

God is a king. He is the Lord of Lords and King of Kings. He is our Father; He created us and breathed into us the breath of life. This has made you a Royal Priesthood. In fact, you are a person of distinction, live like Royalty, in other words you can't speak defeat.

We don't speak failure, we speak Victory, and Royals are over comers. We speak with power and authority for we represent God on Earth. Did you know that every king needs a priest? Watch on any major function crowning kings and leaders like presidents. There is always a priest to lead the function even on a wedding ceremony.

Priests have a special role in every part of life, from family, business, politics, government, cultural and social structures, bringing solutions to the world.

The world is waiting for the manifestations of the sons of God.

Royalty is in two forms; natural birth right and God given power. It is through believing Jesus that we obtain power to become sons of God. Understanding who you are will help you in whatever you speak and think steps in your mind as what a man thinks so is he. Proverbs 23:7

Matthew 7:12 says, in everything, then, do to others as you would have them do to you. For this is the essence of the Law and the prophets. Claim your heritage, you belong to the Royal class. We have received a free gift but it's up to us to believe it, receive it and walk in the power and authority.

Royal law is a very fitting label since this command comes from the Lord, our King and the highest of all Royalty or Nobility. The Greek word basileia translated as Royal in this passage from James in the KJV appears only five times in the New Testament, always related to the status of Royalty or nobility.

The "Royal Law" which is referred to in the new covenant is expressed in the Ten commands which Yahweh spoke into existence as a revelation of the nature of God and the way for man to live in harmony with Him. The Ten Commandments came from a King and is worthy of His Kingdom (James 2:8-12). God has never done away with His Ten Commandments, and they never shall be done away. They will be lived by all those given eternal life forever.

It is for this purpose that the written word serves as a means of exposing the works of the flesh to us now. It acts like a mirror to reflect the image of God to us, a measuring stick with which to compare ourselves.

So that if we lose sight of the image of the new 'man', by looking into the "perfect law of liberty", it will be reflected back to us to expose the works of our flesh (James 1:22-25). James calls it the "Royal Law". In Psalms 2:7 we read, "I will declare the decree: The Lord hath said unto me, thou art my son; this day have I begotten thee." Ask of me and I shall give thee the heathen for thine inheritance, and the uttermost parts of the earth for thy possession.

It went further and says thou shall break them with a rod of iron; thou shalt dash them in pieces like a potter's vessel. Be wise now therefore, O ye Kings: be instructed ye judges of the earth.

Beloved, let's begin to claim our heritage, we belong to the Royal class. We break the yoke of second-class citizen and such mind-set be broken in Jesus Name. May your life begin to shine the Glory of God.

Royal Civility

Royal Civility is a personal decision to believe and follow the laws and guidelines God has given us. Walking in your divine right and authority as a child of God is as simple as receiving salvation.

We are all spirit beings having a human experience on Earth from birth and on day will be required to go back to the Father our King and give a report of how we used our gifts. That is why we need to keep in mind that, our divine Royal Civility can never expire. The good deeds we do on Earth will be rewarded in the eternal kingdom of God. There is no substance in a lone person mentality as we all need each other; therefore, what we need is a civil society. In the Royal civility family, we all have virtues, rights and obligations helping us know how one should live but also how we should live together to cut through religious, political and cultural separations.

The Value of Royal Civility

The value of royal civility allows all children of God with different and conflicting views on life to live peacefully side by side by being respectful and polite to each other. We get to celebrate each other's differences, just like God created flowers of different colours, so is the diversity of all the billions of people.

We are not the same but can live together in harmony and sympathy for others and selfless love.

It's a practice principle of living without violence among nations. Suitable structures like diplomacy among nations play a role in negotiating. Incivility in the world is like the use of loud car horns on a busy day brings a sense of disorder and loss of dignity among people as some shout at each other etc. but this kind of act can be overcome by good manners and etiquette, courtesy to each other.

In God's kingdom, we bear the fruits of the Holy Spirit which helps us to function on earth and be civil. Some of them are, patience, love, joy, peace, righteousness, and joy in the Holy Spirit.

Contribution

A man's gift opens doors to them. The only mirror is the God of the Bible and that is the standard for us. Whatever we do here on earth is a reflection of what is being done in heaven. Our part is to make good choices, because choices are presented to us, and to follow the path laid before us with peace and not anxiety. When we know we are royal, other people seem to know it too.

There's a Kingdom in Africa, called Tooro Kingdom

and were they have the world's youngest king. HRH King Oyo spends almost all his public time at charity events, blessing others, bringing joy to others through charity work, giving finances to the needy and a preserving a good name to the Royal family. If we truly believe we are heirs to heaven, would we spend so much time worrying about little things like finances, our future careers, or what someone thinks about us? No! Knowing how securely placed we are, how loved we are, how provided we are, we would feel more free to use our time to expand the kingdom.

We might be doing the same thing we're doing now, but the motivation and strategy would change and therefore, so would the proceeds. No longer would we be striving for more money, more power, more followers, and more honour or to be "the best." Instead we'd be conscious of manifesting "Kingdom Living" by pursuing excellence in our work and ministries, by putting people before money, by loving well, forgiving well, taking criticism with grace and setting examples with how we love and raise our families.

What percentage of your time is spent being motivated by expanding the kingdom or manifesting kingdom life? What percentage of your time is consumed in worry?

But seek first his kingdom and his righteousness, and all these things will be given to you as well. (Matt 6:33)

Chapter Two

WHAT IS A KINGDOM ON EARTH?

A Kingdom on Earth is a state, territory or government having a king or queen as its head.

Every kingdom must have a king or Queen. A king exercises his authority and influence over a specific geographical area. And a king's sovereignty is absolute. He is not voted into nor out of office or power. His sovereignty is by birth right or in other words, a right of birth. The same is true of a king's lordship, the reason is because all kings are automatically lords. What differentiates a king from other type of human leaders is "Lordship." The reason is simply because the Lordship makes any king unique.

In addition to that, the quality of Lordship distinguishes a king from any top government officials like president, a prime minister, governor or a mayor. I'm emphasising on this term Lordship because Kings personally own the physical domain over which they reign. This is what makes them not only kings but lords too. I could say kings and property go together!

There are two special words being used when referring to kings and kingdoms. The word Dominion can be regarded to the king's power which is his authority. While the word Domain refers to the property, territory, the area over which his authority reaches.

Privileges of Kings and Queens

Let's look at some privileges a king or queen has that others do not have.

The divine rights of any king is God's mandate to them. It asserts that no king (monarch) is subject to no earthly authority, deriving the right to control or rule directly from a divine authority, which is God.

Therefore, the monarch (king) is thus not subject to the will of his people or any other estate of the realm. What this means is that, it is only the divine authority can judge an unjust monarch and that any attempt to dethrone or minimize their powers runs against to the will of the divine and may constitute a sacrilegious act. And it's often expressed as "By the Grace of God", attached to the titles of any reigning monarch (king).

Throughout history, we see different kinds of kingdoms, however, below are certain characteristics common to all kingdoms:

- ✓ A King or Lord —a sovereign and Royals live in palaces
- ✓ A Territory —a domain
- ✓ A Constitution —a royal covenant

- ✓ A Citizenry —a community of subjects
- ✓ The Law —acceptable principles
- ✓ Privileges —rights and benefits
- ✓ A Code of Ethics —acceptable lifestyles and conducts
- ✓ An Army—security
- ✓ A Commonwealth —economic security, and
- ✓ A Social Culture — protocol and procedures

These are certain characteristics common to all kingdoms. Now, we will explain each of the characteristics being mentioned.

The King or Lord

I want us to get this right… being a king is hereditary, birth right, thought to be chosen by our God. We found in the Bible on how kings were chosen and supported by God's providence.

A king is the embodiment of the kingdom, representing its glory and nature. The king gives authority and his word is supreme. Our Saviour Jesus Christ was born as King. You can read Mark 1:14-15. He came as a King and he preached the Kingdom of God… Mark 15:32.

The Territory

As I said earlier, a territory is a domain over which the king exercises total authority. Both the territory property, resources and the people the king has power over them.

By right, the king owns all and, therefore is considered lord overall. Note that the word Lord denotes ownership by right. Lord is only given to one who is sovereign owner. Both a King and a Queen have the power to set punishments for those going against the laws.

The main duties of a king are to defend his realm, keep the law, and to do justice. To make sure that these laws are being followed strictly, the king sent out commissions. And if there should be any disorder it will be reported to the king who then will punish those involved.

The Constitution

The constitution is the covenant of a king with his citizenry which expresses the mind and will of the king for his citizens and the kingdom. The constitution can also be referred to as the documented words of the king, which details his will and mind for his citizens. The king/Queen choose all their advisors and ministers who assist them with the affairs of government. It is the reference for life in the kingdom of God. Matthew 5:3-10 Blessed are the poor in spirit, for theirs is the kingdom of heaven. Our constitution says, "The word of the Lord stands forever" (1 Pet 1:25a)

The Citizenry

The citizenry are the people that live under the rule of the king. Citizenship in a kingdom is not a right, but a privilege, and is a result of the king's choice. The benefits and privileges of a kingdom are only accessible to citizens and therefore the favour of the king is always a privilege.

Once one becomes a citizen of the kingdom, all the rights of citizenship are at the citizen's pleasure. The king is obligated to care for and protect all his citizens; and their welfare is a reflection on the king himself. As a citizen in a kingdom, the number one goal is to be subject to the king, seeking only to remain in right-standing with him.

The Law—The Royal Word

The law constitutes the principles and standards established by the king himself, by which his kingdom will function and be administered. Everybody living in that kingdom must obey the laws which include foreigners residing in it.

The laws of the kingdom are the way by which one is guaranteed access to the benefits of the king and the kingdom. Violations or going contrary of the kingdom law will place one at odds with the king and thus interrupt the favourable position one enjoys with the king.

The citizens have no right to amend the laws in a kingdom nor are they subject to a citizen referendum or debate. In other words, the word of the King is law in his kingdom. Rebellion against the law is rebellion against the king.

The Privileges

The privileges are the benefits the king gives to his faithful citizens. This aspect of kingdom is quite different from other forms of government. In a kingdom, citizenship is always desired by the people because, once you are in the kingdom, the king is personally responsible for you and your needs. In addition, because the king owns everything within his kingdom, he can give to any citizen any or all his wealth as he desires.

A Code of Ethics

This is the acceptable conduct of the citizens in the kingdom and their representation of the kingdom. It includes moral standards, social relationships, personal conduct, attitude, attire, and manner of life. Kings or Queens make all the decisions affecting their kingdom.

The Army

Every kingdom has army as a system of securing its territory and protecting its citizens. It is important to understand that in a kingdom the citizens do not fight in the army but enjoy the protection of the army.

A Commonwealth

It is an economic system of a wealth which guarantees each citizen equal access to financial security. In a kingdom, the term commonwealth is used because the king's desire is that all his citizens share and benefit from the wealth of the kingdom. The kingdom's glory is in the happiness and health of its citizens.

The Social Culture

The social culture is simply the environment created by the life and manners of the king and his citizens. This is the cultural aspect that separates and distinguishes the kingdom from all others around it.

It is the culture that expresses the nature of the king, through the lifestyle of his citizens. Kingdom social culture is supposed to be evident in our daily activities.

God's kingdom Citizens has Legal Rights.

The Kingdom of God is a real kingdom with covenant rights for its citizens it's like a constitution of sort, statues, laws and a kingdom government or a monarchy. And the bible says this government, led by the return of Christ the King and His true disciples (those who obey Christ), will rule over all the nations on earth for a thousand years. "The kingdom of the world has become the kingdom of our Lord and of his Christ," (Revelation 11:15).

Do you know your rights? As a child of God, you have legal spiritual rights, but you have to know what they are to exercise them! As a believer, you are a citizen of the kingdom of God, and you have a right to everything in the Kingdom. There is a covenant between Jesus and God, signed in Jesus' blood, which provides these rights for you. If Jesus is your Lord, then you are in right-standing with God, therefore you have the righteousness of God. You have a right to everything God has.

In life, people are willing to fight for their rights, and what belongs them. They put forth a big effort to make sure they get what is rightfully theirs, for example, an opportunity, a personal belonging, a raise, a promotion. But, in spiritual things, they tend to just roll over and give up.

Kingdom Legal Rights

1. You Have the Right to Be Free "Therefore if the Son makes you free, you shall be free indeed." John 8:36 (NKJV)

When God created man, He gave him the gifts of life, dominion and free will. Why did He give us free will and not just force us to be righteous? Because God didn't want robots or servants. He wanted a family. That's why the right, the privilege and the power to decide has been left by God in the hands of men.

2. You Have the Right to Be Healed. "By His stripes we are healed." Isaiah 53:5 (NKJV)

When it comes to the rights provided by the government, we may have to fight for those rights at times. But with God, you don't have to fight for the right to be healed. No. Jesus has already dealt with that.

You are a son or daughter of Abraham, in other words, a seed of Abraham and you should be healed today. Jesus broke the power of the curse that came on Adam, and if you'll exercise your authority in Christ Jesus by His Name, His blood, His Word and His resurrection, as a joint heir with Him then that curse does not have any legal right or authority over you.

3. You Have the Right to Prosper. "And God will generously provide all you need. Then you will always have everything you need and plenty left over to share with others." 2 Corinthians 9:8. People have the idea that spiritual things are separate from material things. That isn't true. Spiritual laws govern material things. God created all matter.

So, the laws of prosperity will work for anyone who will meet the biblical requirements to walk in them. God has always promised, "If you are willing and obedient, you shall eat the good of the land" (Isaiah 1:19, NKJV).

4. You Have the Right to Use the Name of Jesus. "And this is his command: to believe in the name of his Son, Jesus Christ." 1 John 3:23 (NIV)

We have a commandment to believe on the Name of the Son of God. To believe on His Name is to put demand upon His ability. The mighty, powerful Name of Jesus is available to you. But, you must become aware of your right and privilege to use it.

The Name of Jesus is the key to heaven's storehouse. It can do anything that Jesus can do. Philippians 2:9-11, everything in existence in heaven, earth, under the earth, will bow its knee and confess with its mouth that Jesus is Lord. The Name of Jesus is the Name that is above every other name.

5. You Have the Right to Never Fear Again. "For you did not receive the spirit of bondage again to fear, but you received the Spirit of adoption by whom we cry out, 'Abba, Father.' Romans 8:15.

Do you have any fear in your life? Right off, you may think you don't. But, do you worry about anything? Are you afraid of getting sick, getting fired or losing a loved one? Are you afraid people are talking about you behind your back? Are you afraid of what your future looks like?

Let's start here: You have the right to never ever fear again. God didn't give you a spirit of fear, He gave you a spirit of power. When you're empowered, you don't fear. Fear isn't natural, and it isn't responsible. It's nothing but torment (1 John 4:18). And Jesus didn't come so you would be tormented but He came to give you dominion, authority, peace and perfect love. The word says perfect love casts out all fear.

Chapter Three

BORN TO REIGN

If we truly understood who we are in Jesus and what He has done for us, Christians would be the most confident people on earth. Insecurity would be banished from our lives forever. We'd reign in life as kings. We'd walk around on this planet like we own it. Why? Because, the fact is, we do through Jesus.

God blessed them and said to them, "Be fruitful and increase in number; fill the earth and subdue it. Rule over the fish in the sea and the birds in the sky and over every living creature that moves on the ground." Genesis 1:28

This is what God pronounced upon man after he was created; the same voice that said "let us create man" was the same voice that blessed him with the power of dominion. God designed that man should rule totally over the earth, over everything He had created, and that was why everything in the garden bowed to Adam and Eve when they were still in tune with God. Not even lion nor tiger could look them in the eyes even though they were not physically armed. They carry the kind of glory that no creation can challenge. It was obvious that they were gods on earth then.

The Psalmist confirmed in Psalm 8, that God had put all things under the feet of man, and had given him dominion over all the works of His hands. What a wonderful revelation.

The truth is that God has not withdrawn this statement. The decree that was made in creation is still in force, but something else happened that set it aside. Man fell by eating the forbidden fruit; thereby surrendering the authority that God gave him to Satan. But God made a promise right from the Garden of Eden that the seed of the woman, Eve, will bruise the head of the serpent. This meaning that the seed will destroy the power of Satan. That seed is Jesus, the Saviour of the world. For this reason, the son of man is made manifest to destroy the works of the devil (I John 3:8).

Jesus came to restore what we lost in Adam, and He did a perfect job of it, in a way that it cannot be reversed. Now we have the authority and dominion that Adam had and lost in the garden, but only in Jesus.

For as many that have given their lives to Jesus Christ, they have that power in them. We are more than Conquerors through Christ that loved us. Greater is He that is in us than He that is in the world (I John 4:4). Christ in you the hope of Glory (Colossian 1:27). That is why believers in Christ can cast out demons and they will obey them. They have that authority of Christ backing them.

If you have not known Christ, if you have not surrendered to Him, you can do it now.

Right where you are, cry to Him to save you. Confess your sins and forsake them, you will obtain mercy, and receive your dominion back. Say with me, Father I come before you, forgive me of all my sins and come into my heart. I receive you and believe in you. In Jesus Name. Amen

As joint heirs with Jesus, we are the seed of Abraham. We are inheritors of the Blessings that made the whole world his possession through Christ Jesus (Galatians 3:29, Romans 4:13). This earth belongs to us just as surely as the Promised Land belonged to Isaac back in the day when God said to him: "Sojourn in this land, and I will be with thee, and will bless thee; for unto thee, and unto thy seed, I will give all these countries, and I will perform the oath which I swore unto thy father Abraham" (Genesis 26:3).

In the Hebrew language, to sojourn in a land literally means "to walk around and dwell in it." He told Israel to go in and possess the land. That's what God expected of Isaac and what He expects of us. He doesn't want us walking around helpless, like trespassers, on this earth. He doesn't want us limping along, hoping for a little bit of blessing now and then. He wants us to sojourn with boldness, believing every day of our lives that He is performing for us the oath He made to Abraham.

He wants us to act like what He told us in the New Testament is true: "All things are yours; and ye are Christ's; and Christ is God's" (1 Corinthians 3:21, 23). He wants us to operate with the carefree confidence of beloved children who know their Father meant it when He said, "Surely blessing I will bless thee, and multiplying I will multiply thee" (Hebrews 6:14). Most people, however, can hardly imagine such a life. We've been too religiously brainwashed. We've been told too often that you can't get God to do anything…that He doesn't perform His oath anymore…that we have to live like beggars on this planet because "you just never know what God is going to do." The Bible says that when he saw Jesus, he "fell on his face, and besought him, saying, Lord, if thou wilt, thou can make me clean" (Luke 5:12). That man had no idea that, as a descendant of Abraham, healing and every other aspect of the Blessings already belonged to him. So he approached Jesus with an awful sense of insecurity.

Even though he knew Jesus was a prophet of God, even though he recognized the Anointing that was on Him and believed that Jesus could do what he was asking, he wasn't sure if He would. But, thank God, Jesus didn't leave him wondering. He settled the issue not just for the leper but for all of us by saying, "I will" When Jesus said those two words, He wasn't just responding to one man's need. He wasn't saying, "Yes, in this particular case, it's My will to heal." He was saying, "I will perform the oath that my Heavenly Father swore to Abraham." Jesus is the same yesterday, today and forever (Hebrews 13:8). God never changes (Malachi 3:6). If it was His will to perform the oath of Blessings a few thousand years ago, it's still His will right now. If it was ever His will for His people to sojourn, it's still His will today. Equal Partners with Jesus and Joint heirs to Gods kingdom.

Chapter Four

PRINCIPLES OF A KINGDOM

In this chapter, we are going to talk about those principles that all kingdoms operate and provide for the well-being of its citizens.

The Kingdom Economy

Every kingdom operates on a system that secures and sustains the power and viability of the kingdom. The system includes the kingdom governments' providing opportunities for its citizens to participate in the benefits program of the kingdom's prosperity by contributing to the work ethic and culture of the kingdom. Taxation system, investment opportunities and creative development programs for the citizens are those things involves in the kingdom economy.

The Kingdom Taxation System

All kingdoms incorporate a tax system, which enables the citizens to take part in the process of maintaining the kingdom development like infrastructure and other things that could bring development to that kingdom.

It also allows its citizens to share in the kingdom's commonwealth and return set part of the kingdom's resources back to the monarch (king). However, everything within the kingdom belongs to the king, such as the taxes required from the citizens. In regard to that, taxation is the government's allowing its resources to go through the hands of its citizens.

Delegated Authority

In every kingdom there must be a representative system that delegates responsibility to appointed citizens to serve as ambassadors and envoys of the kingdom.

Ambassador does not care about their own personal needs but they personify and embody the king's authority and kingdom. They are the property and responsibility of the state. Their main purpose is to represent the interest of their kingdom.

In addition to that, the kingdom ambassadors speak for the kingdom and they do not represent themselves but only the kingdom which they are assigned to represent.

The Kingdom Administration

Whether small or big kingdom, they do establish a system through which they follow to administer their judgments and programs to the citizens. This program is designed to guide the rights and privileges of its citizens and their access to the kingdom's favor.

Worship

This is an indication or expression of the citizens showing gratitude and appreciation to their king for all his has done for them, such as his favor, security of being in the kingdom and other privileges.

It can also be in a form of offerings or gifts to the king, indicating the citizen's awareness that all things he or she enjoys are the pleasure of the king and the acknowledgment that everything belongs to the king.

Lastly, worship also expresses a citizen's dependency on the king, which makes the king to care more for the citizens who proclaim his name as their king.

The Kingdom Education

In every kingdom there is a system and program for training and educating its citizens. The purpose of the educational system is to re-enforce, transfer and inculcate the laws, morals, values and matter of the king and the kingdom to succeeding the upcoming generations.

Influence

All kingdoms must be committed to make the influence of the king and his will felt all over the kingdom.

Decrees

A royal decree is simply a declaration of a king that becomes law to everyone within the kingdom. It is sustained by the king's personal effort to bring the declaration to pass.

Royal Favor

This is the sovereign prerogative of the king to extend a personal law to a citizen that positions such a citizen to receive special privileges and benefits that are personally protected by the king himself.

Reputation

Reputation is very important to the king and is the source of glory of his name. It's created and sustained by the conditions and the citizens and his kingdom. So, he acts in ways that are favorable to their name's sake.

Giving to a King

Giving to a king motivates the king's obligation to show his glory and strength to the giver and to prove that he's a greater king than others. Giving to a King shows that the citizens are grateful and they believe that all things belong to the King. Giving benefits the citizens more than the king. That is why you need to activate the act to receive blessings.

The difference between a Royal Mindset and Religion.

- Religion controls man with laws and punishment, the Royal mindset allows repenting and being righteous through Christ.
- Religion prepares man to leave earth while the kingdom of God empowers man to dominate and rule earth.
- Religion focus on heaven and hell, Royal mindset focuses on bringing heaven on earth.
- Religion is limited, Royal mindset is unlimited we can do all things through Christ.
- Religion is attached to certain beliefs and practices and Royal mindset believes in the work of the Holy Spirit sent from God.
- Religion is based on how holy they are and rituals and a Royal mindset is when you have a relationship with God.
- Religion focus on a founder/ mediator to link them to God and Royal mindset is seeing God in everyone as created in his image.

The Culture of Royal Civility

Chapter Five

HOW TO LIVE IN THE KINGDOM OF GOD

Living in the kingdom of God is very simply, but you must acquire: Salvation, Sanctification and Baptism of the Holy Spirit. Those things make you a citizen of the kingdom of God.

In this kingdom, God is our everything, such as our Father, Commander in Chief and relies on us his beloved children to represent him here on earth and destroy the work of the devil.

John 17:15, we are meant to be the greatest positive influence on earth. In darkness is where light shines brightest. These are the Rights and Benefits of being a child of God. God wants His Kingdom to be established in every nation to influence every sphere and realm of society.

When God speaks we can't vote and negotiate to where we are assigned in this world, all we have to do is have faith in him that all things are working together for our good. As a child of the King of Kings and Lord of Lords, you have rights and benefits of being a member of the Royal Family of God and this is how that can apply to your life.

Discovering who you are in Christ and taking your place in the Kingdom of God.

When your soul is aligned with God's promises and purposes, you can possess your destiny and live in the perpetual blessings of God

The constitution of the kingdom is the Bible. It contains the benefits and privileges of the Citizens. Matt 6:31-33. Earth was given to Man to manage – Psalm 115:15-Every Kingdom has territories, In the Beginning God Created the heavens and the earth. The first thing God gave man was territory. Let them have dominion. By Prayer we invite God into our domain. We have dominion authority. "Bind" lock up or prohibit, "Loose" Unlock or permit, Matthew 18:18 Land. Domain, Territory Isaiah 45:1822.

You Are Not Meant to Live in Lack

Our Savour Jesus Christ came to this world so that the thief and the devourers would be destroyed and you could know and enjoy abundance in life. This abundance of life includes provision, healing, protection, promotion, deliverance, breakthrough, and many more.

God will not only prosper us but He has given us the tools we need to lay hold of abundance right now. Look at what God did for Abraham, Isaac and Jacob.

The main purpose of this book is to help you open your eyes to God's prosperity plan for you and gives you powerful scripture-based decrees to open heaven's windows of blessing over your life and your immediate ones. The bible tells us that God's word will never returns void. Grab hold of these decrees and get your financial breakthrough.

But to be part of all the benefits, you must make sure you accept Him as your King and Lord. Lord demands worship. The gospel of the kingdom has showed us that Jesus should be Lord of our lives, and the Bible should be the guide for every kingdom citizen.

We must have the right mental understanding to operate successfully in the kingdom of God. One of the common things among us is that the kingdom of God is not a democracy, neither a denomination, however, a theocracy governed by the King of Kings and Lord of Lords. This is simply a sovereign rulership. The different between the sovereignty of God and man is that, there is no voting and no protests. Yet, there is still freedom through Jesus Christ.

Only in the kingdom of God you can liberty without voting. There's peace and it is not a prison; it's divine protection. In other to achieve the fullness of being kings and priests, we must get it right how kingdom authority operates. If you want to understand this better, you can find the story of the centurion in Matthew 8:5-10.

This man came to Jesus to ask Him to heal his servant that was sick "And Jesus said unto him, I will come and heal him. The centurion answered and said, Lord, I am not worthy that thou should come under my roof: but speak the word only, and my servant shall be healed. For I am a man under authority, having soldiers under me."

He had authority because he was under authority. If you want authority in the kingdom, you must be submitted to authority. Again, the kingdom of God is not a democracy, it is the life of God.

We can't predict on what the kingdom agenda will be. In the kingdom, one accepts the rule of God in their lives and enters into the realm of His blessings here on Earth. At the heart of submitting to kingdom authority is whether or not a person is truly surrendered to the Lordship of Jesus Christ.

When you accept Jesus as your Lord and saviour, then you come under His authority to do the things that He says. At this point we can see that, the kings and priests pattern has both Godly and worldly versions; but the worldly version is a counterfeit of God's true pattern and is always inferior. We all know that Pharaoh and Nebuchadnezzar were both powerful kings and formidable rulers, but they knew there was a realm in which they were not graced to function.

This is a good revelation. Understanding their own limitations, they had spiritualists advise them on things pertaining to the intangible and invisible spiritual realm. Today, we still have the principle of kings and priests' active operation. For instance, many tribes still practice ancient tradition where the king or tribal leader routinely consults their priests, who are called the witchdoctors or soothsayers (sorcerers).

They are in partnership to rule over the personal and corporate affairs of the tribe or business ventures. In fact, today, the common practice is for people to employ the soothsayers and spiritualists to consult "the spirits" for answers about things like businesses, political matters, marriages, families, and other things they may be going through.

And people pay thousands of pounds or dollar for their consultation services. This is the worldly way of kings and priests. However, it illustrates what I'm driving out that there is power or strength that results from this union.

Lots of tribal nations know the benefits and authority of these kings and priest's relationship and see results, even if limited. These countries, whether big or small, have talented people who contribute greatly to their country's phenomenal development or growth. Recently, there was an article released by a local newspaper in one of those countries that said a student at one of the major universities can earn a degree in astrology and land prestigious jobs with well-known multinational corporations and financial astrology websites. These people are being hired as financial astrologers to make predictions. The reason I'm saying all these is to clear your mind that the kings and priest's principle is alive and still being used in this twenty-first century.

Any wisdom aside of God's wisdom is regarded as counterfeit wisdom today. This counterfeit wisdom so to say is inferior, and consulting any medium, soothsayers are forbidden by the Lord, as it was very thing used to tempt mankind in the Garden of Eden. For instance, Pharaoh's magicians and soothsayers were only able to go far in executing Spiritism in their efforts to duplicate the power of the Living God though Moses. As we read in the Bible, no enchantment can compete with the finger of the Almighty God. Another incident was during the time of Joseph and Pharaoh's astrologers when they could not predict the 7 years' famine. The intelligence of the Egyptians couldn't avert it.

The Culture of Royal Civility

Chapter Six

ROYAL PROTOCOL

In 1 Corinthians 14:40, we read that, but all things should be done decently and in order. Now, let's take a look what protocol is all about.

According to Webster's dictionary, a protocol is a code of ceremonial forms and courtesies of precedence accepted as proper and correct in official dealings, as between heads of state and diplomatic officials.

We are going to concentrate on this definition.

Therefore, a royal protocol is an art of bringing divine order and alignment among the children of God. A royal protocol is a reference to the respect, honour and deference due over all times to those in authority in the different levels of leadership.

It is also a tool and guide to assist God's children in embracing the Biblical mandate for divine order in all areas of their lives. It has helped to removes chaos in the manifesting of the Kingdom of God on earth. By following these principles, we walk in a realm of light, love, prayer and also divine order.

Here are types of Protocol
Law of Subjection to Our Leaders

The Almighty God has called us to be subject to one another in love…read 1 Peter 5:5. It's an attitude of heart; actions alone will not constitute submission. You can be doing the right deeds, however, if your heart is rebellious or if we think bitter through toward one whom we are serving, how can we then say we are truly submitted?

The Bible says God looks at our hearts and not our deeds. Although pure deeds come from a pure heart, they alone will not constitute purity before the Almighty God and our follow human being.

Every authority that exists has been ordained by our God. So, when we resist authority, we are in reality resisting God. Sometimes, this is as a result when earthly powers are opposed to God. But we should first submit to God. Note that, without higher powers, or where there is no authority in place, anarchy reigns. For example, if a father does not exercise dominion in his home, the mother might come in instead to rule, creating a matriarchy.

The Lord takes that pyramid that organizational structure that man has built and He says, oh, what an interesting picture of greed and hatred or He turns it the other way round! In the church, the leaders are the foundation, which is the bottom of the pyramid. Instead of them being served, they serve. Instead of occurring honour, they honour and bless others.

Family Relationship

None of us chose the family into which we were born. As a little child, you probably didn't say I'm no longer wish to be a part of this family or I resign. So, I will be part of the next door family. However, sometimes due to challenges you might have felt like it.

That's why it's necessary that we look more deeply at what family and relationship is all about. The first thing that comes to mind is a family begins with a couple (newly wedded couples). And when these two people become parents, they automatically become authorities as well.

They take actions and oversee the demarcation of boundaries of such action, and the children are responsible for being subject to them. But if we believe in the sovereignty of God, we will be able to stand and work out any issues that arise, knowing that it's He who put us there for a purpose and that we that we are not released until He says so.

Protocols / Etiquette in the modern-day Kingdoms.

Every Royal family operates under a completely different set of rules, etiquette, and traditional protocol. For instance, these policies and procedure are meant to maintain a certain amount of decorum and respect for their positions. People from all over the world looks to the British royalty for proper manners, and they expect nothing but the best.

Royal Honor

Being around Royalty is, for many, a once in a lifetime event. If you're ever invited to a royal event, remember that it is a huge honor, so brush up on your etiquette and enjoy. The memories will be with you for the rest of your life. Unlike other invitations that include a request for Reserve and give you the option of declining, an invitation from the monarchy is more of an order than a question. Even if you don't want to attend, you'll always be able to look back on the experience and brag about it to your kids and grandkids.

General Key etiquette and protocol for Royal families across the world are as follows.

1. Do a study about the culture and language of that

kingdom. For instance, it's against British Royal etiquette to kiss the Queen but the Spanish King did just that when the pair met.

2. Dress professionally or be Modest in Appearance while meeting the ruler. It's believed that we all need to dress as we want to be addressed.

3. Follow the Leader. When you're in the company of the Royals, wait until she or he sits before sitting. When they stop eating, follow the lead too and put down your fork. If you're ever in doubt about what to do, look to the Royal for guidance, just do what they do and you can't go wrong.

4. Curtsies, Bows or kneeling for women it was expected for citizens under their royal reign to curtsy or bow it's a respectful gesture while greeting. Keep the curtsy subtle and the bow in good taste to make it appear that it comes as second nature.

5. Hand shake for men, when greeting royalty is recommended, you'll need to give a firm and gentle hand shake. If you don't have confidence in doing this, practice before you find yourself in an embarrassing situation makes direct eye contact and smile. Being friendly is always in style.

This rule does not apply to when you're around the Queen of England. You shouldn't make any attempt to touch her, even for a handshake.

6. Conversations with the Royals. Before you join anyone in the royal family; prepare to listen more than talk. Create a few easy subjects and questions. E.g. talk about the weather and other harmless subjects. Don't get into anything that is controversial, such as your views on politics, religion, or other topics that can start a debate.

7. Don't sit as long as the Royal is still standing. After the royal sits down, go ahead and follow suit. One of the most important things female royals learn is how to sit. It's important to keep the legs together, particularly when wearing a dress or skirt. Don't cross one leg over the other at the knee. If you need to cross something, do so at the ankles. Practice this position in front of a full-length mirror before going to a royal event.

8. Give plenty of personal space. Never be so bold as to touch a royal after the initial handshake, unless she initiates the contact. Only other members of the royal family may place a hand on them. Of course, this excludes members of the medical community when they are called on to heal the Queen or deliver one of the royal babies.

9. Always take a gift to a Royal on your visit. It's a

good habit to cultivate to impress someone. It's always graciously accepted no matter how small it is.

Civility Humanitarian

Civility is defined as polite act, caring or expression. Humanitarianism is simply an active belief in the value of human life, whereby humans practice benevolent treatment and help other humans, in order to better humanity for, moral and logical reason.

Focusing on civility in any area you find yourself, is important to make the world a better place to live in. Focusing on communication and addressing misunderstandings and conflicts are important to avoid chaos.

Aside what we have mentioned, civility means a great deal more than being nice to one another. Civility is complex and encompasses learning how to connect successfully and live well with your neighbours, developing thoughtfulness, and fostering effective self-expression and communication.

Chapter Seven

THE KINGDOM PRINCIPLE OF MANAGEMENT

The world leaders are beginning to feel the real effect of the global economic crisis, in this period of corona virus all over the world. The European report is not exciting at all. And the United State report showed that people who are living on $1 a day has jumped from 2 million to 7 million, and those living on $2 a day will jump from 3million to 9 million which means that poverty is expanding.

The leaders all over the world still don't know the way out… if the leaders are guessing the followers are in trouble. Everything seems glomming and everything is predicting crisis. However, let me just say little about the crisis, Gods economy is never in crisis. We as royalty are the solutions to the world.

A crisis is an event over which you have no control. The way you get ready for crisis is you the event under your control.

That is why usually, crises are experiences you don't prepare for didn't anticipate…that is why they called crisis. So, the way you minimize crisis is to always be preparing for the unexpected and expected. Take not of this.

The Keys to Overcome Crisis

- The Kingdom Citizens Are Not Immune to Crisis

One thing that is important to remember. Because you're living in God's kingdom does not isolate you from unexpected and uncontrollable events. So set that in your mind.

- The Storm Will Hit Everyone

Jesus made this clear when He talked about those who built their house on His word. He said the storm rose, and waves blew and they hit both houses and so crisis affects everybody. But he did talk about the response of the two houses and one of them crashed and the other stood firm because of the foundation.

Survival Will Depend On Your Foundation Knowledge

Remember He said anyone who hears my words and put them into practice will be like a man who built his house on a rock and when the storm blow, wave rise and water comes, that house stands firm. So, it was not the storm that was the problem, it was the foundation that was the problem. If it wasn't the right foundation, then you have a problem.

So, crisis is not the problem. They are going to come to everyone, the only difference is how you deal with it. Problem is what you have inside you to handle the crisis.

I want you to stop thinking like religious people and start thinking like Kingdom people.

Religious people look for miracles. They want God to take care of them without their efforts; they are lazy! They want magic supply, they want immediate response from God and if God delays, they stop believing in Him. This religious spirit is a dangerous spirit and is very.

- Management Is The Key to Prosperity In Poverty. I put it to you friend that, management is the key to prosperity in the middle of poverty.
- Management Is The Key To Promotion In Crisis

Do you know that people are going to get promoted during the next few months? Some people will be laid off and some get promoted…watch! And some folks will get more money far than what lazy people gets. They get jobs that lazy people are laid off from.

And people who are good managers will be

promoted! God does not promote you because you pray, neither does fasting bring promotion. Promotion is the result of management.

- Management Is The Key To Power In Crisis

If you want to be the person controlling positions in mist of coals, you must be the one who has good management skills. No one wants to lose a good manager, so if you aren't being a good worker before you must change that attitude right now.

Your pastor can be praying for you to get a good job, but if you aren't hard working and a good manager you will be on the back seat.

God promises crisis…you know we have been told this funny idea that God is a good God. We only say God is good. So, God does good things. I remember one day I was reading the Bible and I saw this young man who walked towards Jesus and said good master sent from God, and before he could make the next statement, Jesus stopped him and said; excuse me, why do you call me good? But when I think of it one should be happy when someone calls you good. Christ stopped him, why do you call me good? Before he could answer Christ answered. "No man knows what good is only God."

I was a teenager when I got the key. Therefore, from that day my definition of good was cancelled because I don't know what good is only God knows what good is. Because what you know is good may not be good and what may be bad may be good in God's plan.

So, God is making a promise to the nations of the world that crisis is coming, and He tells the leaders before it happens. If we read Genesis 41: 25-27, And Joseph said unto Pharaoh, the dream of Pharaoh is one: God hath shewed Pharaoh what he is about to do. Joseph was 17 years when he began to make an impact in the land of Egypt. This is Joseph the prince in Egypt. The famine God was talking about is economic crisis. In those days, the economy was built on agriculture so the worst thing for those countries was farming. So, that is a problem because people don't want to spend money.

Chapter Eight

ROYAL CIVILITY QUOTES

Julian Businge Quotes

1. A kind gesture is ultimate respect for humanity
2. Royal Civility calls us all to lead by example in this life
3. Gratitude is a choice that can open doors
4. A Royal civility culture is bringing heaven on earth.
5. Royalty is a state of mind where you allow yourself to be and have all the good things you deserve.
6. The thing that everyone desires and wants is for their efforts to be recognised and rewarded.
7. Being Civil starts with being nice to yourself
8. The ingredients of Royal Civility are being nice, respectful, and kind to humanity.
9. Nobody is a no body, everyone is somebody.

Sir Clyde Rivers Quotes

- Give civility a chance to solve your problems. I have a solution.
- Views differ because of different experiences.
- Governments govern, ideas change the world.
- Change starts with me. I Choose to make peoples life's better every day.
- Unique people may not see things the same way but we can be kind to each other
- Some conversations are not to win they're for learning
- Civility can never take a day off. So, let's work it
- We teach Civility here…. the future begins to look a lot better…. Children are 100% of the future…. Civility for all
- I have a Solution…
  We don't have to agree on everything, but let's agree to be civil.
- Never be distracted by the noise….
  Do the vision
- We can solve all of our problems.
- The creator loves his creation
- Nobody is a Nobody

- God made man in his image. No more the King has spoken.
- I need you to win so we all can win
- Not afraid to confront the old to build the new.

Royalty Affirmations

- I allow myself to walk in kingdom authority
- I am Heavens' representative on earth
- I give myself permission to be and do everything God has purposed for me
- Heaven knows my needs and I shall not lack
- Today I recognise my divinity
- I am a divine being having a human experience and am enjoying it
- I am leading with my gifts
- Today I choose to seek first the kingdom of God and his righteousness.
- Today I activate my gifts to serve
- Am doing great works through Christ
- My Faith makes me whole in Spirit, Soul and body
- Am born to make positive impact everywhere I go
- I am a child of God
- Am beautiful just like my creator
- Blessings are my divine inheritance
- I am a first class Citizen
- I am chosen
- I decree as a king and pray as a priest
- Am not afraid

- Am divinely guided
- My life shines the Glory of God

ively engaging young people in productive networks around the world, the time has come to chart new directions for the future. Through the Foundation, His Majesty has established a truly global network of institutions and communities, schools and training centers, conservation and educational programs.

Chapter Nine

GLOBAL INITIATIVE

Royal Branding International

Our aim is to help personalities, businesses, and various especially African kingdoms tell their authentic story. This story will allow them to rewrite their future on a local, national, and international level.

Our current project since 2019 is working closely with HRH King Oyo Nyimba and HRH Queen mother of Tooro, Queen Best Olimi in Uganda to create unique Royal fashions and designs. This is aimed at blending tradition and modernity and create modern-day cultural wear.

With our international work with Kings like Omukama Oyo of Tooro: The World's Youngest Ruling Monarch as recorded in the Guinness Book of Records; African Queens and Princesses; Ministers and Ambassadors; celebrities and many other personalities.

Our services will give you the confidence needed to discover your Royalty, re-right your life and rewrite your future. Our services are provided through consultation and mentorship with our Founders and Global Partners:

Dr. Julian Businge: Royal Fashions Expert, Royal

Ambassador at Large Global Relations, and Business Strategist.

Dr Patrick Businge: Founder of Greatness University, Royal Ambassador at Large Global Relations, Special Advisor to Monarchs, and World's First Rewrite Your Future Expert.

Ambassador Sir. Clyde Rivers, Our Patron, Global Partner, Founder of I Change Nations and a leading global voice in the World of Peace and Civility.

We believe that we are all ROYALTY, we just have not yet walked in it. There is nothing painful than having untold royalty buried inside your soul. Your royalty is too valuable that it should not go unnoticed when you are gone. Your royalty is your legacy. Your royalty needs to be told, written about and monetised.

How Are You Going To Do This? Here Is How.

- ✓ Royal Fashions
- ✓ Greatness Research & Publications
- ✓ Royal Tours
- ✓ Royal Studies
- ✓ Royal Civility show and Awards

Royal Fashions

We will help create your own fashion line. This will allow you to dress in your own brand and make your own mark in casual, official, and ceremonial settings.

We will also create bespoke products to match with your brand such as watches, ties, shirts, stationery lapel pins, house hold items etc.

Greatness Research & Publications

We believe that greatness leaves footprints. That is why we are the world's first institution dedicated to discovering, unlocking, and monetizing greatness in individuals and institutions.

Our focused and accessible research makes a difference in any areas of life. For example, we have researched the world's number one motivational speaker Les Brown; the multi-millionaire businessman Antonio T Smith Jr; and the great religious leader Archbishop Doye T Agama.

We have also helped religious institutions capture their greatness in books like 'The City of Refuge Changed Our Lives'. We have researched and documented the greatness of Tooro Kingdom in Uganda and written a Royal Biography for the World's Youngest King.

Let us help you write it, publish it, and share it with the world. We will help you discover the GREATNESS in your business and how to rebrand it.

Royal Tours

We intend to visit kingdoms around the world. Recently in 2019, a team of 15 members travelled to the heart of Africa where the action is. Most people called it the Wakanda experience.

We visited Tooro Kingdom in Uganda and celebrated the 24th coronation of HRH King Oyo. You will experience the amazing culture and mingle with Kings, Queens, Princes, Princesses, and the locals.

Let us take you to Hakyooto events organised by our royal partners and experience African culture. There you will travel back in time and experience the bonfire: a place where knowledge was transmitted from the old to the young through songs, proverbs, and folklore.

Create unforgettable memories as you travel in the heart of Africa, we offer additional services like photograph your safari and document your story in a book if interested in sharing special memories and adventures.

Royal Studies

Did you know that Article 30 of the UN Convention on the Rights of the Child states that children from minority or indigenous groups have the right to 'learn and use the language, customs and religion of their family, whether or not these are shared by the majority of the people in the country where they live'?

Can you imagine ministers and people in your kingdom learning about their ancient, current, and future royal history? Can you imagine clans and community groups gathered learning and celebrating their culture?

Can you imagine books, apps, documentaries, online exposure, and films about your kingdom? Can you imagine tourists coming from all over the world to study about this kingdom?

This is what we will do: we will create Royal Studies in your kingdom that will help people tell their story, walk out of wrong mentalities, leave the bad past, walk into every season of life prepared, and transition into life.

We will research about your kingdom and give you a report on how to align with the modern day changes and yet remain relevant to its clans, rebrand it, align it with the 21st century community and position it in the global royal news. We also have an added service of teaching Royal Diplomacy and protocol to the visitors from around the world or local community ready to learn.

By the end of the process, we will have had lots of fun, spent time with royals, influencers and change-makers, gone on tour with them, shared your message on the ROYAL STAGES, appear on our virtual WALL OF FAME and be in the royal news.

We at Royal Branding look forward to helping you manifest your royalty, create your best life, and live a legacy.

How my business, innovation and initiative is helping my community and our world.

- Every year, during the black history month, we get into schools and youth clubs and online to talk about African Royalty and its importance to us.
- Promoting cultural exchanges between Africa and Europe.
- Teaching Royal Diplomacy and protocol to the visitors from around the world or local community ready to learn.
- Travel to African Kingdoms and the world.

- Online Show called Royal Civility Show where we get to interview top leaders around the world concerning discovering our divine Royalty.

The solutions we are providing are bridging the gap through education and communication between African cultures and Europe and people to appreciate their self-worth and build confidence.

CONCLUSION

We've come to the end of this Royalty Book "The Culture of Royal Civility." However, I would like to conclude the book by making us understand the purpose of the earth and why you are a heavenly citizen.

It's important to remind us that the Almighty God had a special purpose for creating the earth. In Isaiah 45:18, the prophet told us that, "God himself hath formed the earth and made it; he hath established it, he created it not in vain. "This means, God didn't create the earth because He had nothing doing or for nothing. He had a special purpose for creating it.

Genesis 1:1, in the beginning, God created the heaven and the earth. Now, the heaven is the spiritual realm that is inhabited by God and the heaven beings. The earth is the physical realm where plants, human being and animals inhabit. This is not enough to know the intention of God for the creation of the earth.

From a careful study of the book of Revelation, it's clear that God's presence is in every corner of heaven. The heaven is ultimately indwelled by the presence of God and influenced by His will. Heaven is also where God has His throne. This means, God's presence and dominion is permanent in heaven.

In other words, heaven is occupied by the presence of God or the heaven is perfectly under the government of God. This means, heaven is a kingdom where God reign as the King. But don't forget that the heaven is a spiritual world.

However, God also planned to have a physical world where His presence and government would reign just as it's in heaven. God wanted a physical world where His spiritual reign would be physically made manifest.

This is the intention of God for the earth in which you and I dwell. God wanted the earth to be clothed with His presence and governed by His decrees. God want a physical world that would be a replica of heaven ruled by His will and sovereignty.

These purposes were hidden in the statement which God made when creating man. He said; let's make man in our image, after our likeness: and let them have dominion over the fish of the sea, and over the fowl of the air, and over the cattle, and over the earth, and over every creeping thing that creeps upon the earth. While man is to be the physical medium to establish the intention of God for the earth, the earth is intended to be under two things which are:

- The Image of God
- The Dominion of God

This means, the earth was primarily made to be ruled under God's dominion—leadership through His Image. But, for God to achieve this, He made man (You and I) who He wrapped up in His Image and empowered him through His Spirit to establish His sovereignty on the earth.

The Culture of Royal Civility

ABOUT THE AUTHORS

Professor. Julian Businge

FOUNDER OF ROYAL CIVILITY GLOBAL INITIATIVE. SPEAKER, PROPERTY COACH, AUTHOR AND ROYAL FASHION EXPERT.

Profile

'I am a Royalty Speaker and mentor helping people find their true identity through The Word of God.'

And

"I am a Property business coach and offer mentoring and coaching services to women looking for time and financial freedom".

About

Julian Businge is a successful entrepreneur. She is the Founder and CEO of Royal Civility Global Initiative, a firm that specialises in helping people Discover, Develop, Deliver and Celebrate their true identity through the word of God of who they truly are.

She and her husband are co-founders of several businesses, e.g. Peace Apartments, providing serviced accommodation commonly known as Airbnb. Through this firm, she also offers mentoring and coaching services to women looking for time and financial freedom. Also, Together with her husband co-founded World Greatness Awards.

Julian Businge is a Royal Fashion Expert who is creative, caring and customer focused. Her current project in 2019 has been working closely with the Queen Mother of Tooro and King Oyo, in Uganda to create unique Royal fashions and designs. This is aimed at blending tradition and modernity and creates modern-day cultural wear. She is a published author, Award winning speaker, co-authored many books about, Royalty, property and business and is well versed in both areas.

She has been privileged to be coached and mentored by the great legends of our generation like Les Brown, the World's Number 1 Motivational Speaker and His Excellency Sir. Clyde Rivers, Ambassador at Large for Burundi and Founder of IChange Nations. With their help and support, Julian has gone on to become an inspirational speaker whose message touches people in all areas of their lives. She has spoken for various conferences and has won a speakers Award. After listening to her message, one of her fans commented to her message, one of her fans commented, 'It is because of you I did not give up on life'. She continues to work with people who are seeking to change their life's trajectory and rewrite their future.

Indeed, Julian Businge is an example of selfless humanitarian who is focused on helping people around the world achieve maximum success and live their best life.

Achievements

- ✓ Founder of Royal Civility Global Initiative
- ✓ Aug 2020 Honorary Professor of Royal Civility, UGCSI
- ✓ 2020 World Civility Ambassador
- ✓ 2017 Speaker /Author / coach
- ✓ 2019 Radio presenter
- ✓ 2019 Royal fashion expert
- ✓ 2019 Co – founder of world Greatness Awards
- ✓ 2017 Co- Founder of Peace Apartments
- ✓ 2019 Honorary Doctorate, UGCSI
- ✓ 2020 Great Britain Businesswoman of the year
- ✓ 2020 UN representative for the Peace society of Kenya
- ✓ 2020 Global library of Female Authors

Social Media Links

https://www.royalbranding.org/
Email: joliejasi@gmail.com
Some books Julian Businge has published on Amazon

The Culture of Royal Civility

The Culture of Royal Civility

H.E Sir Clyde Rivers, USA

Sir Clyde is the Founder & President of IChange Nations, World Civility Leader, Ambassador at Large for Burundi, Global Board Chairman of OPAD, and Global Spokesperson for the World Civility Day

His Excellency Sir Clyde Rivers is the President and Founder of iChange Nations™. With its slogan "We Honor Ambassadors and Build Statesmen", iChange Nations is the largest "building cultures of honor" network in the world that recognises individuals who have exemplified extraordinary humanitarian efforts to positively change nations.

Sir Clyde Rivers is also the Spokesperson for the World Civility Day and Community Civility Counts Initiative. As a World Civility Leader and Peace Ambassador, Dr. Clyde Rivers believes that every life is valuable and has been created to bring a contribution to the world. Dr. Clyde Rivers uses the Golden Rule "Treat others the way you want to be treated" as his guiding principle in honouring what is good in humankind through *The Golden Rule International* and his organization, *IChange Nations*.

Sir Clyde Rivers has received awards, honours and held offices including being the:

- Global Board Chairman to OPAD
- Recipient of the Nelson Mandela International Peace Award 2019
- Representative to the United Nations – New

York for the Interfaith Peace-Building Initiative (IPI) and the United Nations Department of Public Information (DPI)
- Representative to the United Nations for the Kenya Peace Society Department of Ecosoc.
- Winning the Presidential Volunteer Service Award 2019
- Recipient of the Creativity United, "We Dream in Color," Humanitarian Icon of the Year Award 2018.

In 2017, Sir Rivers won the United States Presidential Life Achievement Award for over 4,000 volunteer hours of serving the Nation and humanity. He is also the recipient of the Danny K. Davis Peace Prize 2017, U.S. Congressman of Illinois. This annual Congressional Award given for excelling in his field and making a difference in people's lives.

In 2017, Sir Rivers was given the Title of Don/Sir when he was Knighted into the original Kingdom of Guatemala and the great city of La Antigua: the first city established by the Spanish Monarchy. He was knighted by Lord EDUARDO L. PRADO S. the Commodore De Santiago De Los Caballeros De La Antigua Guatemala. Sir Rivers is the recipient of an Honorable Mention for the American Civic Collaboration Award 2017 which celebrates partnerships that strengthen America.

Sir Clyde Rivers is the Honorary Ambassador at Large

for the Republic of Burundi, as appointed by H.E. President Pierre Nkurunziza and Special Advisor to President Pierre Nkurunziza, President of Republic of Burundi Africa.

www.ingramcontent.com/pod-product-compliance
Lightning Source LLC
LaVergne TN
LVHW021405080426
835508LV00020B/2471